Life N
Survivors

Life Matters for Survivors.
Maria Esther Parraga-Shahan

Copyright © 2016 by Maria Esther Parraga-Shahan
Cover Design: akiraGraphicz
Coloring Designs: Daniela Alvarez, dalvarez1403@gmail.com

All rights reserved. No part of this book may be reproduced in any form or by any electronic or mechanical means, including information storage and retrieval systems, without permission in writing from the author.
For information, contact Maria E. Parraga-Shahan at:
meparraga@gmail.com.

The content of this book is for general instruction only. Each person's physical, emotional, and spiritual condition is unique. The instruction in this book is not intended to replace or interrupt the reader's relationship with a physician or other professional. Please consult your doctor for matters pertaining to your specific health and diet.

To contact the publisher, visit
CreateSpace Independent Publishing Platform   www.createspace.com

To contact the author, visit
www.lifemattersinstitute.net

ISBN-13: 978-1537727561I
SBN-10: 1537727567
**Library of Congress Control Number: 2016915885
CreateSpace Independent Publishing Platform, North Charleston, SC**

Printed in the United States of America

TABLE OF CONTENTS

DEDICATION v

ACKNOWLEDGEMENTS vii

INTRODUCTION xi

CHAPTER I: Definition Of Survivorship. Survivor. 1

CHAPTER II: Someone Should Do This ... It Might
As Well Be Me! 5

CHAPTER III: I Survived ... Now What? 11

CHAPTER IV: My promise. My passion. My mission. 17

CHAPTER V: Your GPS To Navigate The Waters Of
Survivorship 21

The Seven Keys To A Thriving Survivorship 21

    Key #1: Gratitude ... It does a body good!! 24

    Key #2: Prayer / Meditation / Visualization 26

    Key #3: Healthy food. Hydration. Let go of toxicity
of all kinds. 28

    Key #4: Body In Motion 29

    Key #5: Contact With Nature 31

Key #6: Socialization / Connectivity 33

Key #7: Managing Our Emotions 37

BEAUTIFUL COLORING DESIGNS 43

JOURNALING PAGES 51

DELICIOUS AND HEALTHY RECIPES 59

RESOURCES 79

ABOUT THE AUTHOR 81

DEDICATION

I dedicate this book to the Holy Spirit, who lovingly wrote it in the pages of my heart. I only transcribed it on to paper.

I also dedicate this book to my mother, Carmen Alicia, who was the greatest, strongest and most loving survivor I have ever met.

ACKNOWLEDGEMENTS

My heart is full of Gratitude to God for this wonderful plan of life He has designed for me. I am grateful for His love, grace and mercy.

To my sisters, my family and to my 95-year-old dad, for always giving me the support I needed and for making me feel so loved.

To my daughters Maria Esther and Carmen Carolina for always being my unconditional partners in each and every one of my projects and crazy endeavors. For coming onboard with me in the incredible adventure of writing this book. And for taking on the responsibility of translating it to English, making sure they kept intact my voice and my message.

To my son Jose Humberto Jr. for believing that I am the most creative person he has ever known.

To my friend Donna Ewing who was ready to jump in and take on the role of editor and proof-reader at the drop of the hat, in the mist of her many responsibilities.

To my friend Kim Wilson, Certified Integrative Nutrition Health Coach, for creating and sharing many of her wonderful, healthy recipes.

To my niece Daniela Alvarez for creating the fun designs for the coloring pages.

To my friends at the Life Matters Support Group from the Leah M. Fitch Cancer Center in Lawton, Oklahoma, for allowing me to come into their lives and share my message of Life, Wellness, Joy and Peace.

To Joshua Rosenthal and staff at the Institute for Integrative Nutrition for providing the tools and resources to become a Certified Integrative Nutrition Health Coach.

To all those who took part in the designing, formatting and printing of this book, and helped me realize my dream of sharing my message with others.

And most of all, to my husband Kim Wayne Shahan for his love and patience, and for providing the sense of security, love and protection for me to blossom.

LIFE MATTERS FOR SURVIVORS

"The most beautiful people are those who have known defeat, known suffering, known struggle, known loss, and have found their way out of the depths.

These persons have an appreciation, a sensitivity, and an understanding of life that fills them with compassion, gentleness, and a deep loving concern.

Beautiful people do not just happen."

— Elisabeth Kubler-Ross

INTRODUCTION

Life Matters For Survivors

Today I started writing this book in Spanish, having made an attempt to write in English. Like any bilingual person, I thought it really wouldn't matter much if I started in English or Spanish, truth be told, thank God I can write in both languages. But after talking with one of my sisters, one of the marvelous women I'll introduce gradually throughout the pages of this book, she made me see that my book is already written in the pages of my soul, and from there I want, and should, translate it here on paper. And the pages of my soul are written in my mother tongue! So today I'm beginning to write *Life Matters for Survivors*.

To you who are beginning to read this book, I say that I would have liked to have met you under other circumstances. I wish that our first meeting would have been someplace fun, in the supermarket, at the bank, or that a mutual friend had introduced us. But I know that if you're reading this book it is because maybe, like me, you had or are having a bout of illness such as cancer, or you're facing the loss of a loved one, or you've lost your job, etc. Or perhaps, it is a good friend or relative who is dealing with this tremendous experience of pain or suffering. The reality today is that there are about 13.7 million cancer survivors in the

United States, and it is estimated that by the year 2020, that figure will reach 18 million. So this tells us that cancer is a disease that affects us all, either because we suffer it, or because we know someone close to us who has it, or worse, someone we know and love has died of cancer.

As a survivor of breast cancer for the last 12 years, I want to share with you some advice that has helped me through those years not only to survive, but to have a full life with joy, peace and inner satisfaction -- a life where I look for balance and daily learning, where little everyday things become the catalyst for inner change and reassessing habits and lifestyle. I want to write for you, reader friend, from my experience and my journey with other female cancer survivors who, like me, have set out to start a new stage of life and make that quantum leap into wellness, joy and inner peace.

But as I said, this book is not just for cancer survivors. I think we are all survivors of something. We survive each day, despite our anxieties and fears, in spite of our mistakes and grievances. Despite it all, we are still here. And we ask ourselves this question: I survived…now what?

Many times I have wondered what is that "something" that occurs within ourselves and motivates and prompts us to change. What the mechanism is that prompts us to change and to say "No more!" "This has to be different!"

In my personal case I believe that mechanism was that I got tired of suffering. I also got tired of being a victim of circumstances and a victim of others. It was that "no more," together with the need for self care and protection at a time when I was feeling so vulnerable, that motivated me to change my attitude toward life. It was when I saw myself sick, physically deteriorated, and even more, when I saw my two teenage children filled with fear and anguish not knowing what was going to happen or how to help me. It was at this moment that my mind and my whole soul understood that something needed to change.

Is this your moment, too?

Did you get to this book because someone who loves you and wishes the best for you put it in your hands? Is it just curiosity that got you to glimpse at these pages? Whatever the reason, I want to tell you that just the fact that you are thinking about changing, of longing for a change to take place in your life's circumstances is already a step forward in this process of change and transformation. But we have to do the job. It is the "process" what moves us towards "progress." It is day to day.

It is understanding and recognizing that our habits and lifestyle were established and settled as patterns over many years, not just from one day to the next. Likewise, to change these patterns and lifestyle it requires you to make the decision to change and get on board with this process daily -- little by little, one day at a time.

My change started exactly that way, with little steps every day, walking slowly, but surely. In *Life Matters for Survivors*, I want to introduce you to *my* GPS tool, seven keys that have helped me become a thriving survivor for the last 12 years.

I invite you to continue reading so that I can share with you what has become my promise, my passion and my life's misión.

"You gain strength, courage, and confidence by every experience in which You really stop to look fear in the face."

— Eleanor Roosevelt

CHAPTER I

Definition Of Survivorship. Survivor.

It is difficult to define survivorship, aside from the simple explanation of being the moment when a person is still alive after an illness diagnosis and treatment. Some people consider as a survivor the one who continues living after receiving the diagnosis. The National Cancer Institute (NCI) considers that survivorship starts at the moment of diagnosis and continues for the rest of the person's life. In the medical community, many define a patient as a survivor from the moment he or she is diagnosed. For other medical professionals the patient is not considered a survivor until the cancer treatment is finished. Some others define a patient a survivor 5 years after the treatment is over.

My definition of survivor is the one who keeps on living after diagnosis. I also want to include in my definition those who have survived something which made a profound and deep impact in their lives, those who have overcome tragic or traumatic situations such as the loss of a loved one, physical or emotional abuse, divorce, broken heart, etc.

However, in this book I will refer to survivorship as the time that starts after finishing the treatment. It is in this moment when the treatment ends that we are no longer in a "controlled" environment, where life moves among labs, doctor's visits, treatments (whatever it is: chemotherapy, radiation or any way of natural/holistic treatment). It is during this period that we are on our own, and when I believe we have to reevaluate our life and redefine our lifestyle.

I remember that it was in the period of time when my visits to the hospital ended that I started to feel that everything had changed. I, personally, had physically changed, but I also noticed a deeper change. I felt like I had to do something, that I had to take control of my life and become the owner of my own health and well-being. And even though this sounds very important and interesting, I felt very frightened by the thought of not knowing if I was going to stay healthy or if cancer would return to my life. I believe this doesn't just happen with cancer survivors after the treatment is finished. I believe it also happens to people after a divorce is finalized, or after the funeral of a loved one when suffer such an irreparable loss.

Now we ask ourselves "what should I do with all the pieces of the puzzle I am holding in my hands?" "How can I build everything again?" "Will I go back to my old life pattern?" "What comes next?" Right here is where I found myself 11 years ago. Of one thing I was certain, my life would never be the same, and not necessarily because I had "a bad life." My life would never be the same because I had changed in the process. Now I felt a compassion toward people that I had never experienced before. Now I viewed life as a special and valuable gift. I don't think I had stopped to think this way before. Now I was more aware of what my body felt and experienced. Am I tired? Am I hungry? Do I feel lonely and depressed? Do I need to breathe clean air? What is this sadness sensation that I feel? It is this period in my life that

I want to share with you the lessons and life skills and tools that led me and guided me. I started by listening to what my body asked for or felt. It made me be more in communication with myself and this led me to an introspection and to an interesting journey in my soul and my heart.

If you meditate a little on this, then you will see that we have all survived something that many survive every day. It is to this big set of survivors to whom this book is addressed, for you who have survived and are out there wondering "now what?"

What I lay out in this book is that you are going to start a new phase in your life where you must necessarily go from being a victim of circumstances to being the protagonist, the hero of your own new life. It is not about what happened anymore; you must leave that behind. It's about what can and will happen. We will either be crawling in life because of sorrows, suffering and confusion, or we are going to fly to where our dreams and desires want to take us. It is our new mindset toward this new life we have now that is going to determine our altitude and will take us to claim ownership of our lives and wellness.

Maybe pain and suffering have been your companions lately. I believe now is the time to look at them face to face, to thank them for what they taught us, and to finally let them go. We do not need them anymore. It is through this process of transformation, not just information, that we can see how what once was the cause for pain and suffering, now becomes the catalyst for change, moving us forward and into a life of peace, joy, inner-satisfaction and love.

You are a survivor. A thriving survivor!

> *"Why don't you start believing that no matter what you have or haven't done, that your best days are still out in front of you."*
>
> — Joel Osteen

CHAPTER II

Someone Should Do This ... It Might As Well Be Me!

When I sit down to reflect and look back on the last 12 years of my life, I see a lot of events and occurrences. Some are unpleasant; others are incredibly beautiful and wonderful. It's been almost six years since I came to live permanently in the United States. I am happily married and enjoying peace and harmony in my life.

When I first came to the city where I live now, I felt a little strange and out of place. I didn't know anyone, and I had a bit of a hard time adjusting to living in a small town after having always lived in big cities. So I looked around to see where I could volunteer. I had worked as a volunteer in a cancer center in Caracas and also in Houston. I started volunteering in the cancer center in my town, visiting patients in the infusion room.

But soon I realized that something was missing. I realized I wanted to share a message of life and wellbeing that I carried in my heart. I thought maybe someone should create a support group for women who survived cancer. It would be good if someone could talk to them about the benefits of healthy eating, gratitude, managing emotions, etc.

Years before, when I was going through cancer, I found myself looking around trying to find anyone who could help me survive. I asked myself the question, "Who will do this? Who will bring this message of wellbeing, joy and peace?" Eventually, I realized that the someone I was searching for would have to be me. And that's what I've done for the past five years. I started a cancer support group for women. The promise that once I made myself to take care of myself and never abandon myself, I now extend to other women survivors and share my message of survival and wellbeing.

This personal promise has been made collectively and is a fundamental part of who I am and what I do. This promise has become my passion and my mission, and this book is a vehicle to share this message.

We have survived! We are here! We will create the best version of ourselves! And we will no longer talk of mere survival; we'll talk about super-survival and wellbeing. Wellbeing is nothing more than the sum of a lot of being good -- being good in the physical, being good in the emotional, and being good in the spiritual. We will take the reins and responsibility for our own wellbeing.

Let me take you through a typical day in the life of a successful, prosperous and happy survivor:

One Day In The Life Of A Thriving Survivor

Before getting out of bed, I spend about ten minutes giving thanks to God for this new day that he offers me. I give thanks for my family, my husband, and my children. I also give thanks for the great opportunity to share and help others improve their overall quality of life. Then I do some stretching exercises and finally get out of bed!

I drink a small cup of water with lemon. Depending on the time of year, I drink it hot or at room temperature. This helps with digestion and elimination of toxins, and it's perfect for helping skin look radiant. My breakfast usually consists of a green smoothie (usually with spinach and kale) to which I add protein and organic coconut cream.

Then I drink a cup of coffee with almond or coconut milk, sweetened with a little Stevia. I share this coffee ritual with my husband every day, then we pray together and enjoy our time of communion with God. Even when I'm traveling, I try to keep this same ritual and connect over the phone with my husband if he is not travelling with me, in order to pray together. This is a very important time for us both, one which we give priority to in our daily lives.

Then I check my email, and I'm ready to start the day. I usually try to go out for a walk outside, even if it's only 15 minutes, just to get out in the sun and fresh air. If I have to work away from home, I take and shower and get dressed and go to work. I'm always back home around midday to make lunch. This usually consists of a delicious green salad with mixed greens and spinach, cilantro, cucumber, celery, avocado, carrots, tomatoes, etc. I also add nuts and sunflower seeds. Sometimes I add some organic chicken. I dress it with apple cider vinegar and olive oil.

At least three afternoons a week, I go to the gym for about 45 minutes. When I get back home, I do housework and read or work on whatever project I have. Now that I'm writing this book, I try to devote myself to read or write mainly in the morning. In the afternoon I do revisions to what I've written or answer my emails. When I work on the computer, I mostly do so standing, and I try to minimize sitting for long periods of time.

About three days a week, I train alone at home with weights to tone the muscles in my arms and legs.

I try to eat dinner no later than 7:00 p.m. Dinner is a variation of lunch -- I always have green salad and some vegetables like cauliflower, beets, zucchini, and asparagus, baked with a little coconut oil. Once a week, I eat grass fed, organic meat and prepare my special version of taco salad. Around 9:30 p.m., I start my routine to get ready for bed. I usually take a shower and drink some turmeric tea with ginger and little honey. I go to bed and give myself a foot massage. This relaxes me a lot and quiets my mind.

I try to read before bedtime. Usually I read passages from the Bible or something spiritual so that the last messages my mind processes before sleeping are uplifting, positive, and peaceful. I rarely watch television, and when I do, it is to see a funny or fun movie. By 10:00 p.m. I try to be in bed and ready to sleep! Those who know me know that after 10:00 p.m., I am no longer effective, and that my eyes almost close themselves when bedtime rolls around. My routine of sleeping at least eight hours every night is something that I protect fiercely and to which I give priority. Sleeping well has helped me a lot, and because of it I wake up every morning refreshed and rejuvenated.

This is my day! What is yours like?

Each of us is a UNIQUE being. You should never compare yourself to anyone else. There is no one like you, so I recommend that you develop your own routine, one that will work for you and bring you wellbeing and balance in your life. Obviously, there are practices that are healthy for everyone, but I invite you to discover your own routing, to find your own lifestyle rhythm and healthy eating that brings you satisfaction, wellbeing and peace.

> *"The Elimination Diet*
> *Remove anger, remove resentment, remove guilt, blame and worry.*
> *Then, watch your health and life improve."*
>
> — Charles F. Glassman

CHAPTER III

I Survived ... Now What?

When we go through a painful, sometimes even traumatic circumstance, we experience some hard time trying to feel "normal"again. And this does not just happen to cancer survivors. As I said before, this book is not only for cancer survivors. I believe that we all are survivors of something: disease, divorce, or even both at the same time, or any other illness, trauma, abuse or abandonment. And if your case is like mine, then you will be empathetic to others in a deep and real level. I want to share these lessons and learnings that I am convinced can apply to SURVIVORS in general, no matter what it is that you have survived.

I believe that the first step to claim ownership of our health and well-being is to understand that now you must start over. The life you had before, good or bad, is a closed chapter and a new outlook opens in front of you. You have changed physically, as well as emotionally and spiritually. The person that is here today, reading these pages (or me as I am writing them) is not the same one who was before, and this offers a great opportunity for change -- change of life, change of attitude, change of patterns. This can sound like a lot at the one time, and it can even sound overwhelming. In order for us to claim ownership of our wellness we have to understand that wellness means BEING WELL in the different areas of our life. It is necessary that this new life that I am taking about has to touch and embrace us physically, emotionally and spiritually.

Taking over the responsibility of your own wellness might sound a little intimidating, but only if you think about it like something that must happen from one day to the next. Of course it is not like that. Now you will start a wonderful process of change, day by day and step by step, where effort and progress are not measured by someone else, but by yourself. It is here where you began to LET GO of things, situations and even people, and OPEN THE DOOR to new experiences and learnings what will contribute greatly to improve the quality of your life in a very comprehensive way. You will now become the painter and the sculptor of a new creation. And believe me, only YOU are able to create a better version of yourself.

This change process starts when we accept the fact that to get different results we must do different things. In other words, if YOUR LIFE before this circumstance, illness or tragedy was guided by and focused on others, there necessarily has to be a change. You are here, holding the reins of your life in your hands. You are in charge! It is wonderful! Your priorities will have to change. You have to become the Number One item in your long list of priorities. And you must understand that in order to be able to care for someone, you must love that person first -- you must first love yourself in order to be able to take care of yourself. Loving yourself means taking care of and honoring the promises you make to yourself.

I remember perfectly that when I started to do a little insight I discovered things about myself that I didn't like that much.

I discovered, for instance, that I always waited to hear what others thought and then I would make a decision, some kind of "collage" composed of everybody else's opinion so that I would never contradict anyone. I always agreed with everybody and that made me feel safe. I started to ask myself questions like, "When was the last time I said I DON'T AGREE?" It was in this way that I realized that I was a pleaser. Even though I didn't contradict anybody, in most cases I was completely contradicting myself. I realized that it was not that others told me what to do; I always wanted to do what I thought others would approve of my doing.

That internal contradiction had brought a lot of stress to my life. There were occasions that I felt I SAID one thing, I THOUGHT another thing, and I finally DID yet another thing, completely different. There was no alignment in my mind, my body and my spirit. And when this occurs, when we are completely misaligned we don't have peace, we are constantly trying to please and not contradict others and we forget our own needs and dreams.

So, I decided that this new life, this new stage of my life had to be different. Taking over the responsibility of my own wellness meant that, first of all, that I had to take care of *me,* and be in peace and harmony with myself before even trying to take care of others. This new way of thinking did not mean a drastic change of personality; I was still MYSELF, only different. I started to say NO when I meant NO. I just expressed my opinion when it was required, and if I sadly didn't agree with others, I just said it. So, little by little, change began to take place. How different it feels when you are in peace and harmony with yourself! The anxiety levels start to decrease and a new peace surrounds you.

Claiming ownership of our wellness starts by honoring and giving value to who we are. We harm ourselves by living a life of pleasing others, and we realize that we don't harm others with words or actions by honoring our own agreements and promises. This first step was so important for me, since I went from being the last one in a long list of priorities to putting myself first in line. I started to be my own Number One priority; I started to pay attention to what my body said. If I felt tired, I took a break. If I didn't feel comfortable somewhere, I didn't go to that place. So little by little, my mindset changed and with it my priorities also changed

Healthy eating became very important to me. My taste for natural and healthy food began to be the protagonist in my life. I learned to cook delicious and healthy meals. The concept of "zero toxicity" was something I took as top priority, so everything that was toxic, whether it was people, food, environments or things, I put them aside. I opened my life to new friendships, people with a positive attitude and peaceful nature. I let go of gossip and criticism, and I welcomed gratitude, collaboration, true friendship, peace and joy. This big change of attitude and mindset has brought balance and peace to my life. And thanks to this, I can say that I have claimed ownership of my wellness and that every day I take control of the reins of my life and my health. I have learned to create the best version of myself! I invite you to join me in this creating process, becoming the creator and designer of the best version of yourself!

Let's get started!

> *"Some people see things as they are, and ask, "Why?"*
> *I dream of things that never were and ask, "Why not?"*
>
> — George Bernard Shaw

CHAPTER IV

My Promise. My Passion. My Mission.

Have you ever tried to remember some specific event that left an impression in your life, but there are some parts of it that you remember clearly and other parts that are a little blurry, and you can't remember them accurately? It often happens to me that I don't remember clearly some episodes of my childhood or my youth. I listen to my sisters tell the stories and I try to remember them, but they are not clear in my mind. However, there are other events of my life that I remember with absolute clarity, as if I were living them in the present.

One of these events that is still alive in my mind and my heart was the day that I looked at myself in the mirror, and I promised myself that I would take care of me and that I would never abandon me the way others have abandoned me. I don't know if you had ever gone through a similar situation, but for me, this feeling of abandonment that I experienced during cancer treatment was definitely the factor that led me to establish a new set of priorities. It was then that I started to realize that I needed someone whom I could trust to take care of me and protect me. While my mind went around and around this thought, I tried to think of whom to trust my care and protection to. After much reflection, I knew that person had to be me!

The personal promise I made that day has been such a catalyst for change that it has taken me to an inner search looking for my truths and belief system.

Thanks to that promise, I understood my role as the owner of my personal wellbeing and the absolute creator of the best version of myself. That was the first step in my process of change, going from being a "victim" to being a winner. However, it was not only for me. During chemo treatment I watched other patients in the infusion room. Some of them were there alone, with nobody to keep them company. I started to wonder about them: "Would they have some caretaker?" "Would there be someone in their lives taking the role of companion, relative, friend?"

Little by little, this personal promise started to become a passion for helping other people. I didn't want to become the World's Super Caretaker; I just wanted to share my story with them and maybe inspire them to become the caretaker of themselves. I wanted to share with them and encourage them to become the ones who know how to honor the commitments they make to themselves, the ones who also know how to satisfy their needs of protection, affection, health and wellness. It was in this way that the promise I made on a personal level became my passion and my mission.

I truly believe this life is not just about surviving. It is about having an enhanced and improved quality of life that brings us personal satisfaction, wellness, joy and inner peace. If I could do it, so can you.

In the next chapter, you will receive the seven keys to navigate the waters of survivorship. They are the GPS that will guide you in this journey. Use them, practice them, and you will see how those turbulent waters that brought pain and suffering to your life, become springs and rivers of joy, fulfillment, inner-realization, wellness, love and peace.

> *"By adding simple habits — sleeping a bit more, moving your body, calming your mind, breathing, playing, serving — you will gradually, day by day, shift into a profound capacity for self-care and healing."*
>
> —Mark Hyman, M.D.

CHAPTER V

Your GPS To Navigate The Waters Of Survivorship

The Seven Keys To A Thriving Survivorship

One of the biggest challenges that survivors face is to try to blend into their everyday living the tragedy that they faced. I know that for many cancer survivors like myself, the stage of life that comes after treatment is not only stressful, but it can also be very fearful and intimidating.

When the treatment for whatever circumstance is over, we feel as if we are walking on thin ice. It is at such times in our lives where fear can become a long-term companion. It is not only the fear that a disease or illness can come back; it can be a fear of living and dreaming again. It is as if we are always checking in with ourselves to make sure we are OK: "I have a headache, could it be that I have something bad going on there?" "I don't want to make any plans for vacation because I don't know if I am going to feel good when the time comes." These are just some examples of the many thoughts that were constantly tormenting me. It is then, when the treatment is over, that we have to start a new phase in our lives. It is this "new normal" that we now have to get used to.

I want to share with you what have been my experiences and what have contributed to give me an enhanced quality of life and to help me navigate these waters of survivorship to the point that they have become streams and rivers of peace, joy and fulfillment. This is what I have called "The GPS of Survivorship." A GPS is a global positioning system device that helps us find the best route that will take us from point A to point B. I make this analogy with a GPS to show you that there are seven keys of navigation that are powerful and are resources that can help you to find the best route that will take you from point A where you find yourself right now, toward point B where you want to go, the destination that is awaiting you. I call this the "going back home route."

Each one of us is a bio-individual. We are not the same, therefore, there is no need for comparison. We are UNIQUE individuals. Our everyday walk and learning process have to individually reflect that. These seven keys that I will introduce to you have become the greatest tool for a thriving survivorship. I invite you to embrace them and apply them in your everyday life. Give it a try!

I don't know if you just finished a treatment of any kind, or if you are a survivor of abuse, neglect or just pain. I believe suffering is suffering, no matter what has caused it. I know about suffering -- I have experienced many forms. That is the reason I have the audacity to write this book and why I want to share with other survivors some of the tools, skills and resources that have helped me during the last 12 years of my life. I understand that maybe what I think was a wonderful and powerful tool, i.e., these seven keys, may not relate or apply to you. However, even if one or two of these keys are not for you, I would like to insist that you at least give them a try.

Give yourself a chance to work with them and discover something new and very beneficial for your life and wellness. Each key by itself it is not what has helped me to thrive and feel fulfilled and healthy. It's the sum of them working together that has become a guide that shows me the daily steps to move forward toward a wonderful life. These seven keys are tools, instruments that you now have at your disposal. If we have a map that shows us the way, we can be sure to get to our destination. If you don't know where you are going, it will be very difficult for you to get there. Let these seven keys be your map. Set your intention to where you want to go!

Now that your treatment is finally over, divorce papers are final, or whatever tragic situation is over with, you are here by yourself. Where do you want to go? What is your life destination? When I asked myself those same questions, I immediately knew what I *didn't* want! I didn't want to be sick, I didn't want to live with the fear of cancer hovering over me. I didn't want to be a victim! Once I knew what I did *not* want, I begin to think about what I wanted and wished for myself! Therefore, I began to study, search, explore and dream!

You can claim ownership of your wellness, but for that to happen you have to make the decision to take one step at a time, understanding that what took many years to become a habit in your life, will not be modified or let go of your life in one day. It takes time, little by little, step by step, until you feel that a new life, the best version of yourself is coming out. This GPS, these seven keys, can be a valuable tool that shows any survivor the best route to go from being someone who survived, to becoming a Thriving Survivor!

Key #1

Gratitude … It does a body good!!

A daily dose of gratitude is one of the most important nutrients that our body needs. I know it can be difficult to even think about gratitude when you are going through or just recently went through something as traumatic as an illness, the loss of a loved one, divorce,etc. I believe that what gave me a little understanding of this feeling of gratitude was when I started to think not about what *had* happened, but in what *could have happened* but God prevented from happening. The worst could have happened but it didn't! Thank God! I started to experience this gratitude in my heart when I saw other patients in my cancer support group who didn't have the financial resources to pay for the medicines that they required. I listened to them talking about their family lives, the missing son who was a drug addict, the sick father they took care of, how they had lost their jobs because of the illness, and now they didn't have money to pay the rent. I saw them arrive alone because they didn't have a companion or a close relative to help them, even on those days when the treatment affected them badly. I started to feel gratitude for having my children and my family there, helping me and supporting me in everything.

Even though I felt sad and alone because my husband had abandoned me in this traumatic moment, I decided to focus my attention and thoughts in the positive, in what was in fact going well in my life. I was grateful to be alive and to have the strength and energy to keep moving forward every day. Gratitude came to my heart!

Holding on to these positive thoughts is an important key in our transformation. It is not about denying the evidence of what is going wrong in your life. It's about concentrating and focusing your thoughts on that which is fine in your life, as insignificant as it might seem. This way, we start to become witnesses of the incredible mind-body relationship, on how our thoughts have great impact in our bodies.

I strongly believe that we have to hold on to the thoughts of what we wish for, long for and want in our lives. Think and concentrate on what you want to see come true in your life, not what is already wrong.

Gratitude thoughts help us to be more relaxed and deal with stress. Gratitude helps us to connect with God and His love and mercy.

As part of my daily routine, every morning when I open my eyes, I dedicate the first 10 minutes of that day to thanking God for everything that is well in my life and for what I know will be great in my life. I give thanks for being alive and healthy. I thank God for the air I breathe. I give thanks for my family, my children, and my current husband. I give thanks for my job. Every morning by doing this gratitude exercise, I start to feel how the peace and joy of God begin to flow through my body, and this prepares me to start my day in a wonderful way.

My gratitude does not depend on the circumstances of my life. I am thankful to God for being alive and for being who I am. Gratitude does very well for my body and my soul. Gratitude has become the foundation of my GPS for a thriving survivorship. This daily dose of gratitude will fill you with peace and love and it will motivate you to share this great feeling with others.

Key #2

Prayer / Meditation / Visualization

Prayer has an important place in my life. When I talk about praying I don't mean any specific religious doctrine. Religion is not my area of expertise, nor is it the intention of this book to cover the topic of religion.

Previously I talked about positive thoughts and how important they are to our health, however, I must say that prayer has taken me to a level higher than mere positive thinking. Prayer leads me into an intimate conversation with God. But more than a conversation, prayer is my communion with God, that act of receiving from my God. I receive and feel His love, His peace, His healing and His protection.

When I'm praying I forget about everything that is around me. My mind quiets down and I feel God's love and peace that covers my mind and body. Prayer is one of the ways of communicating with God, your Higher Self, and through which we establish and strengthen our personal relationship with the Creator of the Universe.

Prayer is a wonderful thing that makes us feel part of a whole with God. To Him we raise up our prayers, say thanks and feel that something infinitively superior to us has a wonderful and divine plan for each and every one of us. We just have to activate it by becoming co-creators with Him in this wonderful adventure that is life.

If you are someone who is not interested in spirituality, then I suggest you to find some practice, meditation, for example, that allows you to relax your mind and feel that space of connection with your Higher Self. By inducing our minds to this state of relaxation and peace, we contribute to decreasing the levels of stress and inflammation in our bodies. Prayer and/or meditation are powerful keys for your wellness.

I also want to mention visualization as another valuable tool for our physical and emotional health. Visualization is the act of creating images in our minds. When we start creating images of a positive things that we wish for and want in our lives, our minds and bodies start to register these images as if they are real. This is the first step in creating the reality that we want in our lives. I remember that every time I was to receive chemo treatment, I started to visualize my body healthy. I visualized every cell of my body glowing and filled with life, energy and health. I visualized myself beautiful, glowing, and healthy!

When we start to positively visualize, our creativity is activated as well. Giving space to this creativity that God has given us is also highly favorable for your health. One of the creative activities that I like and enjoy the most is coloring. It is fun to color!

So visualize beauty in your life. Visualize yourself healthy, happy, beautiful! Visualize how you want to see yourself. Visualize yourself as God sees you, a wonderfully made human being! At the end of this chapter, you will find some beautiful designs for you to start coloring your life. Allow the blacks and grays in your life to give space to a beautiful rainbow of color and light!

Key #3

Healthy food. Hydration. Let go of toxicity of all kinds.

Healthy eating has become one of the most important keys of this GPS. It is one key that has brought favorable and radical changes to my life. Our body has an inner wisdom, a natural instinct toward health because it was designed in such a perfect way that its natural condition is to be healthy, not sick. It is designed to take care and heal itself. For this healing process to happen in our body, it is essential that we have a healthy, clean diet, optimal hydration and a proper elimination of toxins.

When I talk about healthy eating, I mean eating food as natural as possible, leaving aside highly processed foods, the so called "fast food" or " junk food" which is very harmful for your health. In my personal case as a breast cancer survivor, I have completely eliminated processed/refined sugars and junk food from my daily diet.

Scientific studies talk about the connection between processed sugar intake and high levels of insulin to the growth and development of cancer cells and an increased risk of chronic diseases. That's why it's very important to eliminate refined sugar of our diet. Honey, natural cane sugar, coconut sugar, etc, are great substitutes for refined sugar.

Another important aspect of our wellness is proper hydration. Often we feel hungry when we actually are thirsty. That's why it is recommended that when we feel hungry, we first drink water. There are people who live in a constant condition of almost dehydration, because they satisfy the need for hydration with coffee, juice, or tea. Even though these beverages may satisfy thirst, they are not hydrating the body. Our body is almost 65% water and it requires water daily to carry on all its processes and to perform properly. So, drinking adequate amounts of pure water daily is really important.

As we start to pay attention to our body and to listen to what it has to say and what it asks for, we will be more in alignment and balance with our own wellbeing. As important as It is to be well fed and hydrated, it is also very important to eliminate toxins of our bodies.

When I talk about eliminating toxins I refer, of course, to the natural process of elimination that our body must do daily. However, I also mean eliminating toxins out of our minds, relationships and surroundings.

Key #4

Body In Motion
Exercise / Dance

I believe it is well known to everybody that exercise plays an important role when talking about our health and wellbeing. Our bodies are a wonderful design, a work of art of our Creator that incorporates within the design itself all that is needed for the best functioning of this magnificent creation.

Exercise, as such, is one of the many ways we can keep our body active and in motion. Whatever mode of "body in movement" that you choose, you will be positively contributing to your wellbeing and quality of life.

I've already shared with you part of my story as a breast cancer survivor for the last 12 years. The story continues here: I remember that when I was about to finish my chemo treatment, I went to a gym near my house, and there I hired the services of a personal trainer. That was a very hard experience for me, especially at first. I felt like everybody was looking at me – after all, I had lost a lot of weight, I was bald, and I really didn't look good at all! The trainer was an amazing young man. I am very grateful for his kindness; however, he wasn't sure where to start. I looked so thin and fragile; I think he was afraid that I would fall apart at any moment.

At the beginning, I got on the treadmill for 5 minutes at a moderate speed and then we did some weight training. I started working with a little 3 pounds dumbbells! It was the only thing I could lift. Little by little I got my strength and energy back, but most importantly, I felt I was actively doing something for my health and healing. After a few months everybody knew me at that gym. They all greeted me as I came in every day and they encouraged and congratulated me for my efforts. It felt so good! Even today, many years later, I am still friends with some of those wonderful people that I met there, and who without even knowing it, contributed greatly to my healing.

Today my life continues to be active. I walk outdoors for at least 15 minutes a day; I go to the gym regularly and at least three times a week I do some weight training at home.

But the "body movement" that I like the most is dancing. I have invented my own "dance therapy." Dancing relaxes me, makes me happy and makes my body move to the rhythm of the music, moving and incorporating in this workout muscles that I usually don't exercise. Try it out -- dancing is great!

It doesn't matter if you don't follow the rhythm, or don't know any dance moves. Make it up! Have fun! The important thing is to keep your body in motion. Therefore, whatever mode of exercise you choose to do to keep yourself active, do it at least three times a week. Choose something that you like and enjoy! That way, you will start noticing wonderful changes in your energy levels, moods and overall health.

Part of my job today is being a Health Coach, teaching and inspiring other women to improve their quality of life by making the modifications of lifestyle that they need for their wellness. When I talk to my clients about exercise or "body movement" and I see them doubtful or insecure about how to get started, I always suggest dance as a way to keep the body in motion. It is something that doesn't require experience or qualifications as a great athlete. Dancing is for everybody!

Key #5

Contact With Nature
Walks in nature. Sun exposure.

One of the things that help me the most during the recovery process, once the chemo and radiation therapies were finished, was the outdoor walks that I took daily. But it wasn't just walking; it was also feeling myself among the trees and the natural surroundings, admiring the beauty in God's creation -- this magnificent, intelligent design that makes it possible for the grass to grow, the flowers to bloom and the trees to get taller and give us fruits. During that time I lived in Caracas, Venezuela, and fortunately for me, there was a "mirador' or overlook from where you could see the entire city with its houses, buildings and green areas. I could see from the highest point of this overlook our impressive hill "El Avila" in all its splendor and glory. So I would park my car at the overlook and start to walk. I still remember clearly the beauty and majesty of a tree that in Venezuela we call "Trinitaria." Its flowers with intense red, yellow, purple and orange colors impacted me daily and made me feel a close connection and harmony with this outburst of beauty, color, light, energy and life source that streamed from them and surrounded me completely.

Research studies show that walking in nature is very important in helping the body to enter into a relaxation mode and have lower levels of stress, something similar to what I've mentioned about relaxation exercises and meditation. But beyond relaxation, theses studies reveal that when we walk in nature, whether it is a park, a field or the beach, there is no rumination. That means the mind is not going over and over things that are negative or that bring worries like thoughts of pain, fear, resentment, etc. This recycling of mental waste is what has a negative impact in our health and wellbeing. This constant pondering produces stress and brings inflammation to our cells and to our body, and it is this inflammation that brings all types of illnesses.

If you live in the city, you can find the nearest park and establish a routine of walking in nature at least two days a week. Incorporating outdoor walks into your weekend activities will have great benefits for your health.

If you live in the country like me, don't waste a minute and incorporate yourself into this wonderful landscape that surrounds your daily life. Sometimes I don't have the time for a long walk, but I dedicate at least ten minutes to walk among the trees and wild flowers to breathe and to dream.

I also want to make a special note on the benefits of sunlight. I don't mean lying in the sun for hours. I mean the regular and moderate amount of sun exposure, preferably, early in the morning when it is not too hot. This way you will see how your moods improve and your energy levels increase while you are contributing to your body's production of vitamin D, which is essential for our health and emotional wellbeing. The sun's light is also known to kill bad bacteria and to lower cholesterol. I believe that in the same way that plants use solar energy for their chemical process (photosynthesis), human beings can also take advantage of the benefits that the sun's light bring to our wellness. If you live in places with long and strong winters, maybe you can consider the possibility of using one of those special lights that simulate the sun rays and contribute to improving moods during the winter time.

Key #6

Socialization / Connectivity

Human beings are all born with an internal need to connect with one another. This need for connection is evident in a newborn baby. He/she needs to connect with the mother or the person in charge of caring for that baby. As we grow up, this need is still present in our lives. I am not just taking about the superficial socialization we all have with other people. I am taking about being really connected to others.

The whole world is made up of connections, some kind of invisible chain where each link plays an important role in the strength and wellbeing of the whole chain. When we make significant and positive changes in our lives and we begin to see the benefits that such changes bring to us, we are at the same time bringing those benefits to the people around us who are part of our family, friends and coworkers. It is in this way that we begin to see the ripple effect taking place right before our eyes. We are now "under the influence" of our newly acquired habits and lifestyle, and so are our family members and close friends. Transformation is happening on a large scale. Every link of the "chain" is being impacted by the benefits of your new life!

Have you ever thought that you can be the answer to somebody's problem or need? That by offering your smile, sharing your story or just being plain kind to someone, you are now becoming the very thing that person was in need of or has been waiting for? We all need to be connected to and accepted by others. It is this need for connectivity what drives us to engage in relationships and to seek love, support and respect. However, if our family and friends do not share with us the same values and belief system, then the disconnect happens.

Many times when changes occur in our lives because of sickness or other circumstances, we see how this disconnection can happen. For example, if we have started a "clean eating diet," it can be challenging for some of our friends to stay connected with us; they might even see us as "different" or "boring," no longer wanting to be with us. We must accept these changes and understand that in the same way that we let go of some negative habits in our lives and adopted some positive ones, we must also now let go of some people. Some of the old friends may drift away, but new ones, those with the same values and belief system, will become the new links of the "chain of your life." Now each link will help one another and the chain will become stronger and stronger.

In my personal life I had to face this disconnection. When I was going through the cancer treatment I didn't feel like socializing and many of my friends just went away. This can also happen because people don't even know how to approach us anymore. They see we have changed both physically and emotionally and they don't know how to handle that; their own insecurities and fears come to the surface and they choose to stay away from us. Whatever the case, what I am trying to convey in these pages is that this need for connectivity with other people is part of that intelligent design that God had in mind when He created us. We were designed to be connected to one another, to relate to one another, to build friendships, to love and to enjoy being in the company of friends and loved ones.

When I began my chemotherapy treatment, I suffered a lot because of the "disconnect" with my husband, but I was blessed by the love and support of my family and children. During the eight rounds of chemo that I received, each one of my seven sisters took turns being with me in the infusion room when I received treatment. I can honestly say today that these wonderful, beautiful, brave and loving sisters were always supporting and encouraging me. I never felt lonely. My children and my parents were also very present and supportive of me, loving me all the way! I remember that I used to go to each chemo session wearing a new hat each time.

I don't know how or where I got this "great idea" of wearing hats during my chemo treatments! I thought that by wearing a hat, I was somehow taking on the personality or attributes of that hat. You wear the hat, you become it! Therefore, I persuaded one of my sisters who is an expert in the creativity field, to design and create a new hat each time chemo treatment came. So I became Galactic Princess, Light Angel, Invincible Warrior, Joy and Healing, etc. It was great! It was fun! I still remember the faces of the nurses in that infusion room every time I was to get treatment. At first they didn't get the "hat thing," but later it became such a fun game for everyone there, including other patients, trying to guess what the next hat was going be, or what personality it would bring about! This became a new way for me to connect with other people and to experience and accept change in my life.

Something really beautiful and incredible began to happen in my life as I let go of old habits and toxic people. I began to look around me and I saw people in need. At the moment in my life where I felt so vulnerable and even lonely, I began to see other survivors like me, but not only cancer survivors. I began to notice and be aware of other kinds of survivors: women like me, with their levels of stress, fear, anxiety. I thought I had problems, but looking at others I realized there were many others in worse conditions than mine.

That is how I began to connect with some of these ladies, talking to them, helping them in some little way. Many times, it was just sitting down and talking to them, making them smile. A new desire to help other survivors began to take root in my heart. I felt a new kind of connection, a new kind of acceptance to a level I never knew before. My family and children began to see a change in me and they felt very happy and excited to see me smile and dream again!

Nowadays I live in Oklahoma. My children and family are far away from me, but I make efforts to keep our family connection alive in spite of the distance. Moreover, I build new relationships that bring joy and peace to my life. For those of you who have survived divorce, abuse or loss of a loved one, as you read these lines you might feel that you no longer trust people. I just want to say that whoever caused such rupture and disconnect in the past, does not have the power to keep you isolated and disconnected in your future. However tragic and traumatic it may have been, we have learned not to extend the red carpet for people to walk all over us and harm us. By setting up very well-defined boundaries and exercising prudence and common sense, we can begin to open the door to the possibility of connecting with other people. Many times this connectivity can take the form of serving and helping others, and then we begin to see that there is so much need out there, that there are people who need help, who need someone to share with them a little bit of time and conversation.

I invest a lot of my time doing volunteer work, visiting cancer patients in infusion rooms, doing workshops and seminars helping women improve their quality of life and spreading this message of life, wellness, joy and peace. The ripple effect that I mentioned before has become bigger and bigger, and I believe that by writing this simple book, I am making an effort to strengthen the chain of life by adding new links.

To you who are reading this book, I want to invite you to play an active part and to become a new link to this powerful chain of life that brings transformation, wellness, joy and peace to whoever connects and embraces it! I welcome you!

Key #7

Managing Our Emotions

Studies have shown that our emotional state is an integral component of our overall health. We have discussed the importance of healthy eating, but I would like to expand on the relationship between our emotions and how we eat. Our thoughts help regulate our body chemistry, so while we are eating we should avoid talking about controversial topics that bring feelings of anger, fear, anxiety and rage. Even if our food selection is healthy, we can better assist our bodies and the process of digestion by avoiding these types of conversations at meal times. Our ancestors were wise and implemented rituals around meal time, such as blessing the food, expressing gratitude for the meal, and without knowing they were preparing their bodies by allowing stomach acids to start flowing and be ready for optimal digestion.

Just as our emotional state can play a part in our digestion, it is also able to influence and impact our immune system. Psychoneuroimmunology is the study of how the brain, nervous and immune system impact each other. Resentment, bitterness, fear and guilt are emotions that constantly bring thoughts of pain and suffering to our mind. Studies also show that emotional pain creates the same response in our brain as physical pain. Many chronic illnesses are rooted in cellular inflammation, which takes place because of the excess of stress hormones, like cortisol and epinephrine flowing through our bodies. This excess is the result of unresolved conflicts and pain starting in childhood and continuing through adulthood.

This is why we must cling to feelings of what we desire for our wellbeing, leaving behind thoughts of fear and sorrow. I believe thoughts are images in our mind that can be constructive or destructive and can affect our overall emotional state. Personally, I can speak of my emotional state prior to my cancer diagnosis. I lived in a constant state of stress and absolute fear that my marriage would end. That constant stress and anxiety did not allow me to sleep and I started having back and shoulder pain that was unbearable and inhibited my movements. So, when I was diagnosed with breast cancer and my then husband decided he no longer wanted anything to do with me or my illness, my stress levels, fear, anxiety and resentment skyrocketed, so much so that when I began chemotherapy treatments, I had to make an enormous effort just to withstand my pain and suffering. That is when I finally looked myself in the mirror and realized that my life and my reality had changed forever. I came to realize that I needed to change those old habits of being a victim and I had to promise myself that I would change my attitude towards life and my circumstances. I had to become the heroine of my own story.

Something that really helped me back then was writing. I had a journal where I began to write about how I felt and where I vented my frustrations over what I was going through. I decided to explore those feelings or rage and resentment and I started letting go of them. I still have that journal, and in it I wrote letters to people I wanted to ask forgiveness of and to others whom I felt I had to let go of. I wrote lists of people whom I wanted to tell I loved them. I wrote lists of people who I wanted to say goodbye to because I no longer wanted to see them and no longer wanted them to be a part of my life. I wrote incendiary letters where I raged and vented my frustration and anger at how unfair my circumstances were. I still continue this practice to this day. I enjoy writing and letting my thoughts flow freely and I would suggest you do it too. Write for you, to cleanse those thoughts from your mind, to vent and express yourself. You don't have to share your writings with anyone unless you want to.

At the end of this chapter I have included some blank pages for you to use. I would love it if you would use this tool starting now so you can start to feel the incredible freeness that comes from releasing pain, resentment and guilt. Another activity I suggest is coloring. I love doing it and I really enjoy it. It's incredibly relaxing and I get lost in it and even lose track of time. I have also included some coloring pages at the end of the chapter with beautiful designs so you can have fun coloring. It may sound childish, but it is very effective at reducing stress.

Our mind and brain are instruments that God has given us to experience the world around us, but we must control our minds and our thoughts and not allow them to control us.

When we have survived circumstances that are painful, harsh and terrible; our mind suffers the impact of trauma. The feelings of abandonment, loneliness, fear, resentment and guilt can turn into permanent guests in our lives that will continue a vicious cycle of tragedy, illness, pain and suffering. We must begin by cleansing our emotions if we want to be masters of our wellbeing.

One of the EFTs (emotional freedom technique) I have used for years is known as tapping. It is a type of acupressure technique in which the person taps on points in the face and body with their finger tips, to clear emotional issues. It touches specific meridian points on the body while maintaining focus on the issue you are trying to resolve while saying positive results for it. This helps energy flow to get the body to find its balance, reduce the impact of emotional trauma and contribute to healing.

I have personally used this technique many times, on myself and on friends, family members and clients, and the results are very effective. Effective handling of our emotions is key to achieving and maintaining optimal quality of life.

We cannot control our external circumstances, but what we can do is create favorable conditions in our minds that can help us manage and navigate whatever comes our way. You are here. You survived. Now you must choose how you move forward. This is where you decide if you will become better than you were before this event in your life, or bitter over what happened. It's your decision!

True freedom comes from knowing how to use the talents, gifts and tools God has given us that promote and guide us towards a healthy lifestyle that brings us wellbeing, satisfaction, joy and peace.

****

You are now part of this message, and this book is my labor of love for me and for others. It is my simple and practical implementation of what God asks of us: "Love your neighbor as yourself." This act of love for myself, taking care of my health and taking the reins and responsibility for my own wellbeing, I achieve step by step every day, and today I hope you will use it in a practical way, and share it with someone else.

BEAUTIFUL COLORING DESIGNS

MARÍA ESTHER PARRAGA-SHAHAN

LIFE MATTERS FOR SURVIVORS

MARÍA ESTHER PARRAGA-SHAHAN

LIFE MATTERS FOR SURVIVORS

Lion

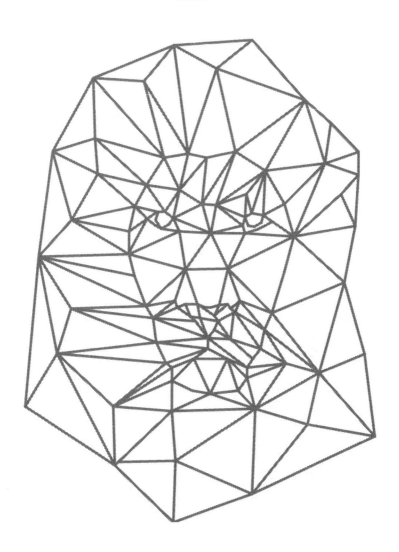

MARÍA ESTHER PARRAGA-SHAHAN

Bird

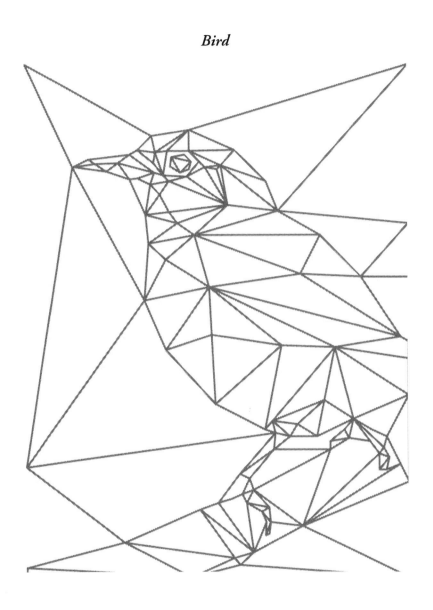

LIFE MATTERS FOR SURVIVORS

Turtle

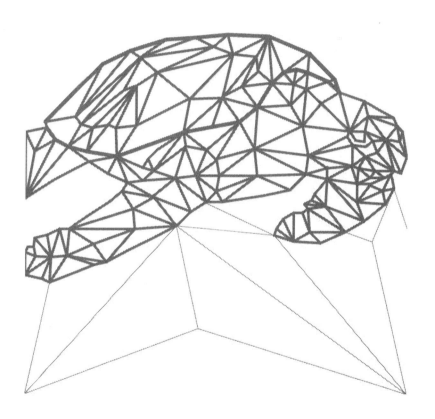

JOURNALING PAGES

MARÍA ESTHER PARRAGA-SHAHAN

PEOPLE I WANT TO SAY GOOD-BYE TO

_____

_____

_____

_____

_____

_____

_____

_____

_____

_____

_____

_____

LIFE MATTERS FOR SURVIVORS

PLACES I WANT TO VISIT

MARÍA ESTHER PARRAGA-SHAHAN

THINGS I WANT TO DO

LIFE MATTERS FOR SURVIVORS

THANKS TO YOU...

MARÍA ESTHER PARRAGA-SHAHAN

I AM GRATEFUL FOR...

TODAY I WANT TO WRITE A LETTER TO . . .

_____

_____

_____

_____

_____

_____

_____

_____

_____

_____

_____

_____

_____

_____

DELICIOUS AND HEALTHY RECIPES

BREAKFAST RECIPES

Chocolate Chia Pudding

Serves 1

Ingredients:

1 cup dairy-free milk
1 tablespoon honey
⅓ cup chia seeds
1 teaspoon cinnamon
2 tablespoons raw cacao powder
1 tablespoon unsweetened, shredded coconut

Directions:

Mix the dairy-free milk and honey together until the honey is dissolved. Next add chia seeds, cinnamon, and raw cacao powder.

Allow the mixture to set for about 8 to 10 minutes. When the pudding is thick, top with shredded coconut and serve.

Cherry Cacao Smoothie Bowl

Serves 1

Ingredients:

1 cup pitted cherries
1 handful baby spinach
1 small banana
½ cup dairy-free milk
1 scoop protein powder
1 tablespoon raw cacao powder
1 handful ice
2 tablespoons hemp seeds
2 tablespoons chia seeds

Blend: Add the cherries, spinach, banana, dairy-free milk, protein powder, raw cacao powder, and ice to a high-speed blender. Blend until smooth and serve in a bowl. Top with hemp and chia seeds.

Berry Sexy Smoothie

Serves 1

Ingredients:

1 cup unsweetened almond milk (or non-dairy milk of your choice)
1 cup organic mixed berries
1 tablespoon chia seeds
1 tablespoon avocado

Note If you're using fresh fruit, add a handful of ice. I like to use frozen berries and keep the additional ice out of the mix. If you want additional protein, add in a clean source of vanilla protein powder.

Mix all ingredients in a blender until smooth. I like to top my smoothies with additional seeds or bee pollen. Enjoy!

Green Love Smoothie

Serves 1

Ingredients:

1 ½ cups dairy-free milk or water
1 cup frozen berries ½ avocado
2 tablespoons chia seeds
1 handful of greens (spinach or kale)
¼ teaspoon cinnamon
4 to 5 ice cubes (optional)

Mix all ingredients in a blender until smooth.

Kale And Eggs

Serves 2

Ingredients:

1 tablespoon coconut oil
¼ cup yellow onion, diced
1 cup shredded kale
Pinch of oregano
Sea salt to taste
Black pepper to taste
4 eggs, beaten

Directions:

Add your coconut oil to a hot skillet and allow it to melt. Add diced onion and cook until soft, about 4 minutes. Add the kale and allow it to cook down, about 3 minutes. Season with oregano, sea salt, and pepper.

Next, add the beaten eggs to the vegetables. Tilt the pan so the eggs spread out evenly. Use a rubber scraper or spatula to turn the eggs over so that they don't harden and burn. Scramble the eggs for 2 to 3 minutes to your desired consistency.

LUNCH RECIPES

Collard Wrap With Tahini Dipping Sauce

Serves 1

Ingredients:

2 collard leaves
2 tablespoons No Bean Hummus (recipe below)
2 tablespoons carrots, shredded
5 to 6 cucumber slices
3 raw apple slices
¼ cup bean sprouts

Tahini Dipping Sauce

3 tablespoons tahini
Juice of 1 lemon
2 tablespoons water
1 garlic clove, minced
Sea salt, to taste

Prepare the tahini dipping sauce:

Add all the ingredients to a small bowl. Mix well with a fork. The sauce should be thin and easy to pour. If it is too thick, add more water. If it is too thin, add more tahini.

Cauliflower Rice Medley

Serves 2

Ingredients:

2 cups cauliflower (chopped)
1 red bell pepper (chopped)
3 carrots (peeled and chopped)
½ mango (chopped)
3 scallions (chopped)
¼ red onion (chopped)
1 tablespoon sesame seeds
1 teaspoon sesame oil
Sea salt and pepper, to taste

To Make the Meal:

Steam the cauliflower until tender, about 10 minutes. Drain and process in a food processor until it reaches a rice-like consistency.

You can also do this raw if raw cauliflower doesn't bother your stomach.

Add all of your remaining chopped ingredients to a bowl. Toss everything together and serve. Top with protein of choice.

Salad In A Jar

Serves 1

Ingredients:

3 tablespoons Tahini Dressing (recipe below)
¼ cup red cabbage, chopped
1 handful spinach
5 to 6 grapefruit slices
5 to 6 cucumber slices
1 handful cilantro, chopped
1 tablespoon hemp seeds (topping)

Tahini Dressing

3 tablespoons tahini
Juice of 1 lemon
2 tablespoons water
1 garlic clove, minced
Sea salt, to taste

Note: If you are not familiar with salads in jars, the whole purpose is to create a beautiful salad stored in a mason jar for convenience. it is important to layer the ingredients as listed to ensure that the salad doesn't wilt before you are ready to eat.

Assemble The Salad:

Use a wide-mouth, quart-sized mason jar. Add the Tahini Dressing to the bottom of the jar. Next, add red cabbage, spinach, grapefruit, cucumber, cilantro, and hemp seeds. Finally, close the jar and store in a refrigerator. When you are ready to serve, simply shake the jar until well coated and eat from the jar, or pour into a salad bowl.

1 tablespoon honey
¼ teaspoon sea salt
¼ teaspoon fresh ground black pepper

Place spinach in a large salad bowl. Chop the cabbage, carrots and avocado chunks. Add the chopped cabbage and beets with the dressing, or simply use olive oil and lemon. Toss thoroughly. Top with protein.

Curried Vegetable Soup

Serves 4

Ingredients:

1 large onion, chopped
1 fennel bulb, chopped
1 pound fresh green beans
1 large carrot, peeled and chopped
1 small yellow squash, chopped
1 large garlic clove, chopped
1 tablespoon curry powder
1 tablespoon dried thyme
1 32-ounce container of organic vegetable broth

Prepare The Soup:

Add all the ingredients to a large soup pot. Stir well and cover with a lid over a medium flame. When the soup is boiling, turn down the flame and let it simmer for about 30 minutes. Puree the soup or leave the soup chunky.

DINNER RECIPES

Healthy Honey Glazed Carrots

PREP: Preheat your grill while you are preparing your food. If you wish to roast the vegetables, preheat your oven to 400 degrees.

Thoroughly scrub your carrots with water. Make sure the carrots are thoroughly dried.

Ingredients:

2 pounds of fresh, organic carrots
Extra virgin olive oil
1.5 Tablespoons of Raw Honey (You can substitute a honey of your choice)

Directions:

Spread your carrots out along the baking sheet or foil. They should lie next to one another and not stack.

First, lightly drizzle your EVOO over your prepared carrots. Massage the oil into your carrots with your hands. Once the oil is thoroughly coated on the carrots, drizzle the honey over top. Massage them around the same way you did with the oil. You want to make sure the carrots are thoroughly coated with both ingredients. Some people like them with a little pepper, but I enjoy them as simple as this.

Spread the carrots side by side on the sheet or foil. Place on the grill (or in the oven). Toss the carrots a couple of times while they cook. This allows even cooking time and prevents additional sticking.

Cooking time is approximately 20 minutes, depending on your desired texture. You can test your carrots by piercing them with a fork. Enjoy!

Farm Fresh Tomato, Basil And Feta Salad

Ingredients:

10 Fresh Roma Tomatoes (chopped)
1 container of feta cheese
Small handful of fresh basil
3 Tablespoons of dry Italian Seasoning (or half of a seasoning packet if desired)
Organic extra virgin olive oil

Directions:

Wash and dice all of your tomatoes. Mix them in a bowl with the feta cheese. Drizzle a small amount of olive oil over your ingredients. Combine and mix in the seasoning. Lay your ingredients out on your serving tray. Sprinkle a small amount of seasoning on top. This may be more than the three tablespoons.

Chill to combine flavors before serving. I recommend a chill time of one to two hours, but it's not necessary.

Serve alone, with veggies or organic pita chips. ENJOY!

Spinach soup

Serves 2

Ingredients:

2 cups spinach
1 young coconut (water and meat)
1 apple, cored and chopped
1 avocado
Juice of 1 lemon
3 teaspoons fresh dill (or 1 teaspoon dried dill)

Blend the soup: add all the ingredients to a high-speed blender. Blend until smooth. Serve in a bowl.

Turkey Rounds

Makes 12 Muffins

Ingredients:

2 lbs ground chicken or turkey
3 egg whites or 2 whites and one whole egg (depending on preference)
1 cup quick cooking oats
1/2 tsp paprika (optional)
1/2 tsp ground cumin
1/2 tsp ground thyme
2 tsp dry yellow mustard
2 tsp black pepper
2 tsp red pepper flakes (depending on preference)
1 tsp salt
2 cloves of garlic (minced)
1 small chopped onion
2 finely chopped celery stalks
Hot Sauce (optional)

Note: As you can see, I add in a lot of options based on preference. I also grate zucchini (a towel helps to remove access water) and diced kale or spinach if I want more veggies. Extra veggies are a great alternative if you want to keep out the oats.

Directions:

Preheat your oven to 375 degrees

Spray muffin pan with a healthy oil option. You can also use a cookie sheet with foil. Make sure to spray the foil to avoid any sticking. I also recommend folding up the sides of the foil.

Mix all of your ingredients until evenly combined.

Form into balls and place in your muffin pan or on foil (evenly spaced apart). This can be done with a small ice cream scoop or large cookie scoop. The rounds should be around the size of a racquetball.

Bake for 35-40 minutes until the meat is fully cooked.

Sometimes I like to drizzle the rounds with hot sauce a few minutes before removing from the oven. This is optional but a delicious choice. Especially if you want some heat. This step is definitely guy tested and approved! YUM!

Serve with a vegetable or healthy side of your choice.

Chicken And Pineapple Skewers

Serves 2

Ingredients:

6-8 ounces of boneless skinless chicken breasts, cut into 1½ inch chunks
2 cloves garlic, crushed
2 tablespoons honey mustard
2 tablespoons tamari
1 teaspoon lemon juice
Salt and black pepper, to taste
1 cup pineapple, 1 ½ inch cubes
1 onion, cut into 1 ½ inch cubes
2 carrots, 1-inch slices
Wooden skewers

Directions:

Soak wooden skewers in water for 30 minutes. Combine the garlic, honey mustard, tamari sauce, lemon juice, salt, pepper and chicken in a bowl and let marinate while the skewers soak.

Preheat the oven to 425 degrees. Prepare the kabobs by threading the chicken pineapple, onion and carrots onto the wooden skewers. Discard the remaining marinade.

Line a baking sheet with tin foil. Place a cooling rack on top. Line up the skewers on cooling rack with about an inch between each one. Bake for 10 minutes. Turn over once and bake for 10-15 minutes longer, or until chicken is no longer pink in the middle.

Lettuce Wrapped Turkey Burger With Broccoli

Serves 2

Ingredients:

6-8 ounces grass-fed ground turkey
1 tablespoon. chopped parsley
1 small onion, diced
1 tablespoon garlic powder
Sea salt and black pepper to taste
2 tablespoons olive oil
1 cup broccoli florets
1/8 cup water
2 romaine leaves (optional)

Directions:

Mix the grass-fed ground turkey with chopped parsley, diced onion, garlic powder, sea salt & pepper in a large bowl and form into two patties

Place a pan over medium-high heat and add 1 tablespoon olive oil, place burgers in the pan and cook on each side for 5 minutes, until cooked through. Once cooked, set burgers aside and add remaining oil to pan followed by broccoli and 1/8 cup water. Let broccoli cook, stirring occasionally until bright green, about 5 minutes.

Remove from heat and serve burger along with broccoli. Burger can also be wrapped in a romaine leaf for added crunch.

Sea salt and black pepper to taste

Salmon With Sautéed Swiss Chard And Lime

Serves 2

Ingredients:

6-8 ounces of salmon
1 tablespoon coconut oil
2 tablespoons water
1 bunch swiss chard, stems removed and leaves sliced into strips
1 lime, juiced
Sea salt and black pepper to taste

Directions:

Turn on broiler or preheat oven to 500 degrees. Season salmon with salt and pepper and place on a baking sheet. Place salmon under the broiler and cook for 7-12 minutes. (7 for medium rare, 12 for well done)

While the salmon is in the oven, heat the coconut oil in a large pan over medium heat. Add the chard to the pan along with 2 tablespoons of water.

Cook, stirring often for 2-3 minutes. Remove from heat and place in a serving dish, add lime juice and toss. Season with salt and pepper. Place the greens evenly onto a plate, top with salmon and serve.

RESOURCES

LIFE MATTERS FOR SURVIVORS

The following books and resources have been an incredible, wonderful source of inspiration, knowledge and transformation in my own life.

After You Ring The Bell... 10 Challenges for the Cancer Survivor, by Anne Katz, RN, PhD.

A Mind of Your Own: The Truth about Depression and How Women Can Heal their Bodies to Reclaim Their Lives, by Kelly Brogan, M.D with Kristin Loberg.

Crazysexy Cancer Survivor: More rebellion and fire for your healing journey, by Kriss Carr.

Eat Fat, Get Thin: Why the Fat we Eat Is the Key to Sustained Weight Loss and Vibrant Health, by Mark Hyman, M.D.

Happy for No Reason: 7 Steps to being happy from the Inside Out, by Marci Shimoff with Carol Kline.

Hinds' Feet On High Places, by Hannah Hurnard.

Integrative Nutrition: Feed Your Hunger for health and Happiness, by Joshua Rosenthal.

Mind Over Medicine: Scientific proof that You Can Heal Yourself, by Lisa Rankin, M.D.

The Tapping Solution: A Revolutionary System for Stress-Free Living, by Nick Ortner

Dr. Joseph Mercola: www.mercola.com

Andrea Nakayama: www.replenishpdx.com

Kim Wilson, Certified Holistic Coach: :www.kimwilson.me

Daniela Alvarez, Graphic Designer: dalvarez1403@gmail.com

ABOUT THE AUTHOR

Maria Esther Parraga-Shahan is the founder and CEO of Life Matters Institute, based in Oklahoma, in the United States. Through this institution she helps and equips women from different strata and socioeconomic spheres to maximize their full potential and transform crisis and poverty into catalysts of change to achieve stability, improve self-esteem and self-sufficiency and enhance their quality of life.

Maria is also a speaker, support group facilitator and a Certified Integrative Nutrition Health Coach, through the Institute for Integrative Nutrition.

Maria Esther Parraga-Shahan is married to Kim Wayne Shahan, founder of *Vision of Hope, Inc.* Both Maria and Kim Wayne perform social, educational, ministerial and missionary work in the United States and in Central and South America.

To write to Maria or to inquire about her speaking services, please contact her at:

Maria Esther Parraga-Shahan
Life Matters Institute
1215 NW Lake Avenue
Lawton, OK 73507

www.lifemattersinstitute.net
www.vohope.org

E-mail: wellnessbeme@gmail.com
meparraga@gmail.com

Made in the USA
Charleston, SC
14 October 2016